AN ALBUM OF
WAR REFUGEES

AN ALBUM OF

WAR REFUGEES

APRIL KORAL

FRANKLIN WATTS
NEW YORK | LONDON | TORONTO | SYDNEY | 1989

Photographs courtesy : UNHCR: pp. 8, 10 (bottom), 46, 49 (bottom left), 50, 52 (both), 53 (both), 54 (both), 55 (all), 56, 64 (bottom left and right), 77 (top right), 79 (both), 80 (all), 82, 84 (both), 86 (top and bottom left), 87 (both), 89 (both), 90 (both); ICRC: pp. 10 (top), 49 (top and bottom right), 51 (all), 59 (bottom), 61 (top); Library of Congress: pp. 12, 15 (all), 18 (top), 19 (both), 24 (bottom left), 58 (top); National Archives: 16, 18 (center and bottom), 20, 22, 24 (top and bottom right), 28, 41 (top); American Red Cross: pp. 25 (both), 26 (both), 77 (top left); UNRRA: pp. 31 (top), 34, 35; Zionist Archives and Library: pp. 31 (bottom), 36 (bottom), 37; UN Archives: 33, 58 (bottom), 59 (top left and right), 61 (bottom left), 62, 68 (top right), 72 (top left and right); YIVO Institute for Jewish Research: p. 36 (top); US Army Photo: pp. 38, 40, 41, 42 (top left and right), 43; Catholic Relief Services: pp. 61 (bottom right), 74, 76 (bottom left and right), 77 (bottom), 78; Defense Department: p. 64 (top); UNRWA: pp. 66, 68 (top left and bottom), 69 (all), 70, 71, 72 (bottom); UNICEF: pp. 85, 87 (bottom right).

Library of Congress Cataloging-in-Publication Data

Koral, April.
An album of war refugees / by April Koral.
p.   cm. — (Picture album)
Bibliography: p.
Includes index.
Summary: Chronicles the plight of war refugees
around the world.
ISBN 0-531-10765-5
1. Refugees—History—20th century—Juvenile literature.
[1. Refugees.]   I. Title.   II. Series.
JV6346.R4K67   1989
325'.21'0904—dc 19   89-30948   CIP AC

TO CARL

CONTENTS

INTRODUCTION

Imagine waking up one morning and not having a home. Imagine being separated from friends, family—even your mother and father. Imagine being cold, hungry, and tired. Imagine being more scared than you've ever been before.

That's what it's like to be a refugee of war.

Each day, there is a war going on in some part of the world. Wars don't just kill soldiers. The bullets and bombs also hit those who happen to be living in the area where the fighting is going on. No one wants to leave his or her home. But refugees of war are usually desperate. They feel that they have no choice. They may have seen an innocent member of their family killed. They may have had their house burned down. They may know they will soon be arrested because someone thinks they're on the "other" side.

Refugees leave their homes with little more than the clothes they are wearing, traveling for days until they reach safety. The trip may be dangerous. Soldiers may fire on them. They may run out of food, or the boat they are in might sink.

There is another side to the tragedy of refugees. During war, there are many acts of kindness. Strangers have protected refugees in their homes—at the risk of losing their own lives. Friends and relatives have helped feed refugees and find them jobs and a new home. In addition to these individual acts, the UN High Commissioner for Refugees as well as numerous charitable organizations help refugees throughout the world. They organize and run refugee camps that feed, clothe, house, and give medical care to people who have nowhere else to turn. They also run schools. Over 50 percent of the world's refugees are children who fled with their parents or alone.

Many countries have also welcomed refugees of war. The United States and Canada have resettled the most refugees. But these nations have not always been so generous. Before World War II, for example, thousands of Jewish war refugees who lived in Europe begged the United States and other

Top: This boy has just arrived at a refugee camp in Thailand, with everything he owns balanced on his shoulders. Bottom: The United States has resettled more refugees than any other country. This refugee from Laos, who now lives in Merced, California, is learning English at school.

countries to open their doors to them. The answer from the world was "no." The refugees were later killed by the Germans.

This book begins around the time of World War I, though it doesn't include all the wars that have taken place since then. Many of the pictures show people who are confused, frightened, hungry, and sad. These people probably feel as if they are living a bad dream. Only when nations learn to solve their problems peacefully will such nightmares ever end.

An Armenian child escaping from the Turks dies before she reaches safety in Syria.

THE ARMENIANS

ONE

"DESTROY BY SECRET MEANS THE ARMENIANS!"

These were the orders of an important government official in Turkey in 1915. The Armenians and their two-thousand-year-old civilization were not destroyed. But some 2 million men, women, and children were killed, and millions more became refugees.

Many of the children of these Armenian refugees live today in the United States. The largest communities are in southern California, New Jersey, and New York, where there are Armenian schools, newspapers, churches, and restaurants. A California governor, George Deukmejian, is of Armenian descent. Every year, the first-graders at a local Armenian school in Glendale, California, plant a cedar tree to commemorate the deaths of their ancestors in 1915. Although the Armenians have become successful in America, they are determined not to forget the past.

For four hundred years, the Armenians, who are Christians, lived under Moslem rule in the Turkish Ottoman Empire. Many of the Armenians were poor farmers; others were business people, craftspeople, government employees, journalists, and poets.

By the late 1800s, a large number of Armenians had become dissatisfied with Turkish rule. Many of them, although they belonged to their own Armenian church, had been educated by Protestant missionaries or had studied abroad. They had learned about democracy and other peoples' struggles for freedom. Now, many of them dreamed of becoming independent of Turkey.

The Turkish sultan reacted to these yearnings for freedom with violence. The massacres began in 1894. Over 100,000 men, women, and children were slain by the Turks; 500,000 children were orphaned or made homeless. Tens of thousands of refugees fled to Russia and Persia, many crossing the frontier on foot during the bitter-cold winter.

The Turks' undeclared war against the Armenians became even crueler after the outbreak of World War I in 1914. Turkey joined the side of Germany against France, England, the United States, Russia, and other European countries. In 1915, the Turks accused the Armenians of helping Russia—and the killings began again.

Nearly 2 million Armenians were forced into the desert by the Turks. The British historian Arnold Toynbee described the fate of these men, women, and children:

> The Armenian inhabitants of the Ottoman Empire were everywhere uprooted from their homes, and deported to the most remote and unhealthy districts that the government could select for them. Some were murdered at the outset, some perished on the way, and some died after reaching their destination. The death-roll amounts to upwards of six hundred thousand; perhaps six hundred thousand more are still alive in their places of exile; and the remaining 600,000 or so have either been converted forcibly to Islam, gone into hiding in the mountains or escaped beyond the Ottoman frontier.[1]

The refugees went to Russia, Greece, and other nearby countries. Some received help from American and British charities in Constantinople, Turkey.

At the end of World War I, the area of Armenia where most of the Armenians lived was declared a country under the Treaty of Sèvres. But the struggle of the Armenians was not over. Tens of thousands of refugees who had escaped the Turkish massacres went to Armenia. They were sick and hungry. But their new country had no money. American and British relief organizations rushed help and medical supplies to the area, but it wasn't enough. An Armenian visitor, writing to an American whom he hoped could help, described the conditions of the refugees:

> No bread anywhere... Not a dog, cat, horse, camel or any living thing in all Igdir region. I saw women stripping flesh from dead horses with their hands today.... Another week will score ten thousand lives lost. For heaven's sake hurry![2]

But it was too late. In 1920, while the rest of the world looked on unconcerned, Turkey and Russia invaded Armenia and ended the dream of the Armenians for independence.

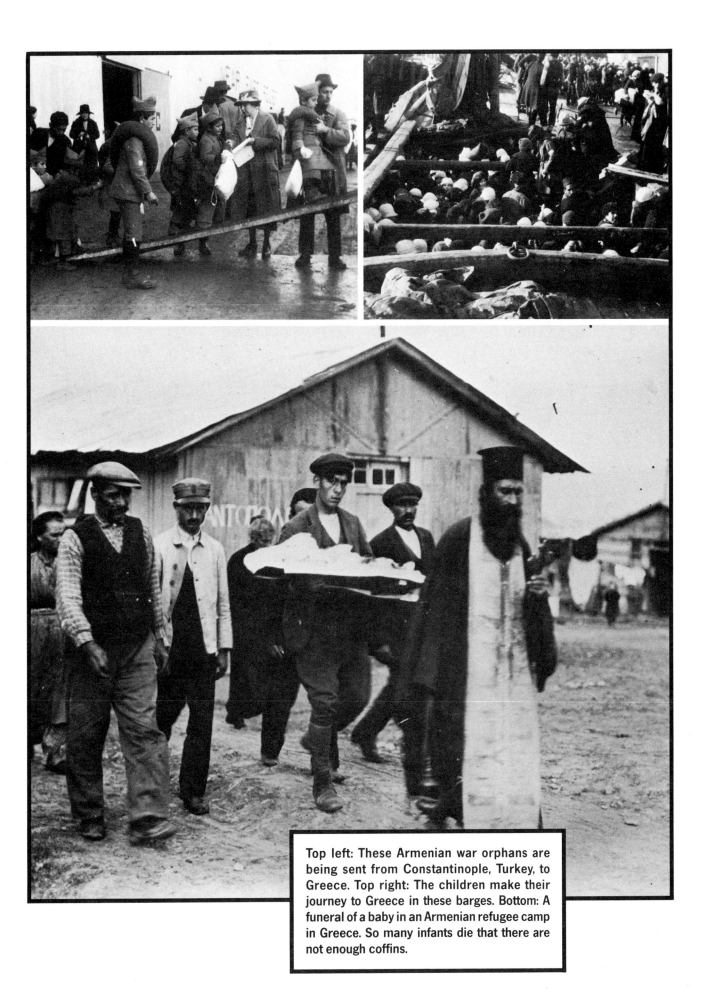

Top left: These Armenian war orphans are being sent from Constantinople, Turkey, to Greece. Top right: The children make their journey to Greece in these barges. Bottom: A funeral of a baby in an Armenian refugee camp in Greece. So many infants die that there are not enough coffins.

A French girl uses a wheelbarrow to carry her sister and brother away from danger.

WORLD WAR I
TWO

It was 1914, and the leaders of Europe were greedily fighting over who was to rule more of the world. Unable to make peace among themselves, they marched their soldiers into the largest and bloodiest war the world had ever seen.

The first shot was fired on June 28, when a lone gunman from the country of Serbia killed the Austrian Archduke Franz Ferdinand. The murder was an excuse for Austria-Hungary to declare war on Serbia. A few days later, Germany declared war on France and Russia. World War I had begun. Before the war ended in 1918, most of Europe and also the United States were involved in the fighting.

As always, civilians were caught in the exchange of bullets. Throughout the war, millions of refugees wandered across Europe and Russia. Some fled their homes with only a few of their belongings wrapped in a shawl or a sheet. Others took a cart or a wheelbarrow. A reporter described one group of French refugees in 1918 as they made their way "very slowly down the highway of war":

> Many children are on the roads, packed tight into farm carts with household furniture and bundles of clothing, and poultry and pigs and newborn lambs. The noise of the gunfire is behind them, and they move faster when it grows louder.... There is hardly any weeping or any look on their faces of grudge against this unkind turn of fate. They seem to accept it with...the most matter-of-fact courage.
>
> Small boys and girls drag tired cows after them. The other day one of these cows leaned against every tree she passed and then sat down, and the girl with her looked around helplessly, not knowing what to do. This morning I saw the girl wearing a veil and

Top: Jewish refugees at the Romanian border;
Bottom: French soldiers with prisoners of war,
and French refugees with all of their possessions loaded on their horse-drawn wagons;

Top: Romanian Jewish refugees line up for food. Bottom: A family of refugees takes shelter in a synagogue in Poland.

Top: These children are homeless and their parents have died. They are waiting for help from the Red Cross. Bottom: Refugees return to their homes in Ardennes, France after the Germans have retreated.

*dressed in an elegant way, taking the cow with her. She was quite
alone on the road. It is queer and touching that most of these
fugitives wear their best clothes, as though on a fete day [holiday].
It is because they are clothes they want to save and can only have
by wearing them in their flight.*[3]

Many refugees were forced from their homes. Germans who lived in parts of
Eastern Europe and Russia were treated without mercy by the Russian army.
Thousands were packed into windowless railroad cars and shipped to remote
parts of Russia. The Jews, who lived in the western part of Russia where much
of the fighting took place, suffered especially. When the Russians were losing
ground to Germany in the beginning of the war, Tsar Nicholas II, who ruled
Russia, blamed it on the Jews. Countless numbers of Jews who lived in
western Russia were expelled from their homes to inner Russia. In May 1915,
all the Jews of Kovno—about 40,000—were told they had forty-eight hours
to leave. The French ambassador in St. Petersburg wrote in his diary this
description of Jewish refugees:

*Hundreds of thousands of unfortunates have been seen wandering
across the snow driven like cattle by squads of Cossacks, aban-
doned in distress in railroad stations, packed in the open on the
outskirts of cities, dying of hunger, of exhaustion, of cold.*[4]

In 1915, there were some 2.7 million refugees in Russia alone. Although the
Red Cross along with private charities tried to help them, they could assist
only a tiny percentage of the needy. One charity had an automobile patrol
that looked for babies who had been left on the roadside by parents who
simply had no food for them. By the beginning of 1916, they had rescued four
hundred such babies. The refugees crowded into the large cities and brought
with them diseases such as typhus, dysentery, and cholera. Thousands of
orphans roamed the country. The refugees had no food and no outer clothing
to keep them warm during the winter.

When the war ended in 1918, most of the refugees went home, though
many returned to villages that had been burned down and farmland that had
been destroyed. Many Russian refugees, however, could not go home. Before
the end of World War I, the Russian Civil War began. Many of the refugees,
along with thousands of newly displaced persons, would not have a place to
call home for many years.

Many refugees were living in a railroad station in Sverdlovsk, Siberia for months. Every day, people with typhus were taken to a hospital.

THE RUSSIAN CIVIL WAR

THREE

For centuries, Russia was ruled by czars. From their vast, treasure-filled palaces, they ran the country with an iron hand. Life for the poor farmers and factory workers in the big cities was harsh, and the average person had few freedoms or rights. During World War I, life became even more miserable as food became scarce and people did not have enough to eat.

Finally, in 1917, the czar was deposed. What followed was a bloody civil war in which the Communist Bolshevik party and the anti-Communists, known as the Whites, fought for power. It ended in 1921 when the Communists won.

In the early days of the war, the educated and wealthy people, who faced imprisonment and death under the Bolsheviks, became refugees. Most thought it was only a temporary move, and they could soon go back home. But many would never see their homes or country again. In 1921, there were nearly 3 million Russian refugees, spread out among every European capital and some cities in Asia. Princesses waited on tables, professors chopped wood. The refugees sold whatever they owned—a ring, a piece of cloth, a jewelry box—in order to eat.

Later, the refugees included those fleeing the Whites as well as the Bolsheviks. Hundreds of thousands of Jews were made homeless by the war as a result of waves of attacks on their communities. In one section of Russia alone, the Ukraine, over 300,000 Jews were killed and over 300,000 children orphaned; another 700,000 were left homeless by the end of the war.

Those Russian refugees who did not go westward to Europe fled north and east. Perhaps as many as a million refugees lived in unheated box cars along the lines of the Trans-Siberian Railroad in Siberia. They crowded into churches or railway stations or tried to protect themselves from the freezing winter by living in dugouts. Other refugees fled south and camped in the streets of Constantinople, Turkey. The Red Cross, the Quakers, and many private charities gave medical aid and set up soup kitchens and orphanages for children who had no parents.

Top: A young refugee is preparing for a bitter-cold Siberian winter by building a dug out — an underground room made of wood and covered with earth. Bottom: A dugout in the middle of the winter.

Top: Thousands of families lived in box cars all along the Trans-Siberian railroad. Bottom: These women and children in Siberia are waiting on the banks of the river for a Red Cross boat to take them to safety.

Top: Thousands of Russian refugees fled to Constantinople, where they ate and slept on the streets. Here, a sidewalk family washes its dishes after a meal. Bottom: The ship leaving Sevastopol, Ukraine was so crowded that some people had to stay in the lifeboats.

Out of the desperate situation of the Russian refugees was born the High Commissioner for Refugees of the League of Nations. The League of Nations was an organization similar to the United Nations. For the first time, the nations of the world took notice of refugees and showed a willingness to help. The League of Nations appointed Fridtjof Nansen of Norway to handle the task. Nansen was a scientist and an explorer who had traveled to the Arctic. Thanks to his efforts, many refugees found jobs and homes and were given loans to help them back on their feet. Many other Russian refugees were given passports so that they could legally emigrate. Eventually, these refugees resettled in forty-five countries throughout the world.

A refugee child receives a biscuit and soup from British soldiers.

WORLD WAR II

FOUR

World War II, the most destructive war in the history of humankind, began on September 1, 1939, when Germany, under the leadership of Adolf Hitler and the Nazi party, invaded Poland. In the next six years, Germany and its allies—Italy and Japan—brought the rest of Europe, the United States, and parts of Africa and Asia into this horrible war. When it was over, millions of soldiers and civilians were dead, and many millions more were wounded.

During World War II, people throughout Europe were on the move, trying to escape from the Nazis. When Italy became an ally of Germany, nearly a million Italians fled the country. In April 1939, when Italy invaded Albania, 3,000 Albanians escaped into Yugoslavia. And when the German army marched into Poland, Belgium, the Netherlands, Luxemburg, and France, over 5 million refugees took to the road—not very safe, since German planes often bombed highways and train stations filled with people trying to escape.

There were also refugees who fled from the Russians. The invasion of Finland by the Russian army in 1939 uprooted 11 percent of the population. And when the Soviet Union marched into Poland at the beginning of the war, it made refugees of an estimated 1.5 million innocent people, shipping them by cattle car to Siberia and other parts of Russia thousands of miles from their homes.

Jewish civilians formed a very large group of World War II victims. Some 10 million Jews lived in Europe and Russia before the war. One of Hitler's goals was to destroy them all. Soon after he came to power, all Jewish businesses were taken from their owners. Anyone who worked for the government who was Jewish or had a grandparent who was Jewish was fired. Jews were stripped of their citizenship. In November 1938, there was *Kristallnacht* ("Night of Broken Glass"), and in one day, thousands of people disappeared into concentration camps, where they were eventually killed or starved to death.

Despite the desperate situation of the Jews before the war, the United States refused to allow large numbers of Jews to come into the country. The few members of Congress who tried to introduce legislation to help the refugees were stopped by others in Congress who threatened to further limit the number of refugees into America or stop immigration completely. Even a bill to bring German Jewish orphans into the country failed to pass.

Why this resistance to Jewish refugees? Polls showed that Americans were worried that the refugees would take jobs away from them. There was also the feeling that America should be for Americans, though everyone—except for the American Indians—had ancestors who were refugees. Finally, there was strong anti-Semitism in the United States.

Ships crammed with Jewish refugees sailed for weeks, begging for a country to let them in. Most never found a home and returned to certain death. Others died in accidents at sea. Finally, an international conference of thirty-two nations called by President Franklin D. Roosevelt met to discuss the refugee problem. It took place in Evian-les-Bains, France. The Dominican Republic offered to allow some of the refugees to move there. Not one other nation would let the Jewish refugees land on their shores.

Meanwhile, in Europe, the Jews continued to flee as the Germans approached. But each time Germany conquered another country—France, Holland, Belgium, Poland, and Czechoslovakia—the Germans either killed all the Jews there on the spot or brought them back to be killed in concentration camps.

There were thousands of brave men and women who helped the Jews. They hid them in their attics, basements, barns, and pig sties. Nuns and priests saved Jewish children by hiding them in convents, monasteries, and religious schools. These people risked their lives, for if they had been discovered, they surely would have been arrested and perhaps shot.

Who were these heroes? They were ordinary people. Some were peasants who had no education. Others were business people, housewives, or diplomats. What made them different from other people was that they felt a responsibility to help others, and they had strong beliefs about what was right and wrong. The people of Denmark, for example, helped save nearly the entire Danish Jewish community. Hundreds of Danes lent their fishing boats, yachts, and ferries and in the middle of the night smuggled nearly 7,000 Jews across rough waters to the safety of Sweden. The leaders of Bulgaria also defied the Nazis, preventing them from shipping 50,000 Bulgarian Jews to death in the concentration camps.

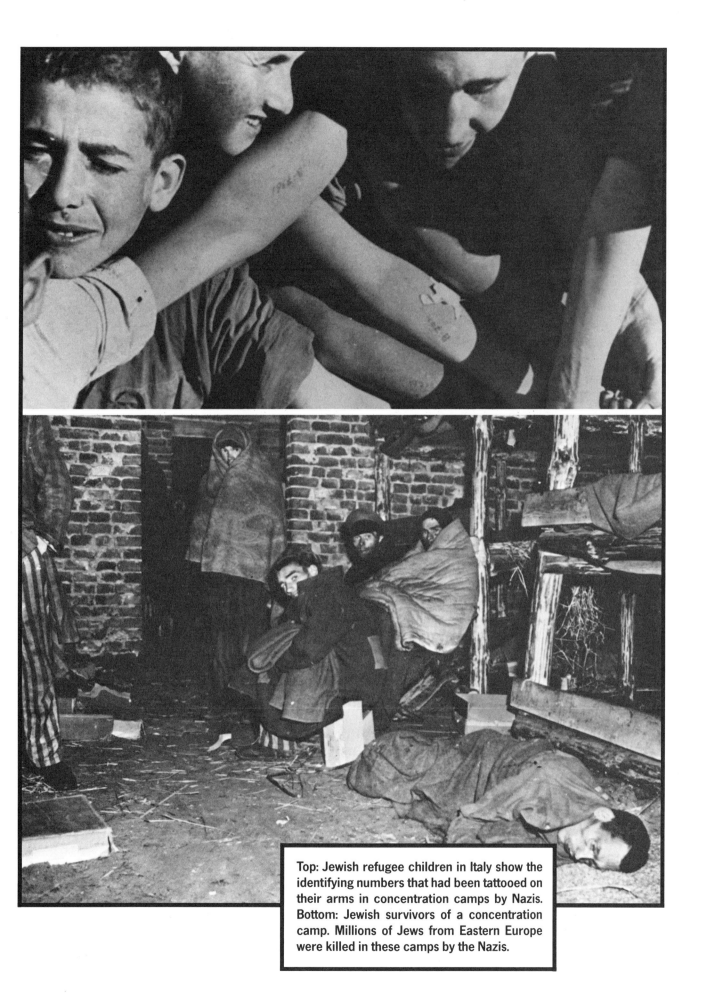

Top: Jewish refugee children in Italy show the identifying numbers that had been tattooed on their arms in concentration camps by Nazis. Bottom: Jewish survivors of a concentration camp. Millions of Jews from Eastern Europe were killed in these camps by the Nazis.

The many refugees who came to the United States after World War II joined in every area of life. Famous refugees included the scientist Albert Einstein, the conductor Bruno Walter, and the writer Thomas Mann. There were refugees who became judges and teachers and business people; others became taxi drivers, factory workers, and waiters. All, in their own way, contributed to their new country.

When World War II ended, there were about 30 million refugees trying to make their way back to their homes. The roads were clogged with people. There were prisoners of war, people who had been forced to work in German factories or coal mines, and others who had fled when the Nazis had marched into their towns. There were also millions of Germans who were forced to leave parts of Eastern Europe, which were given up by Germany after the war. Although these refugees were also often sick, hungry, and homeless, the world had little sympathy for them.

Helping the refugees to return home or resettle in other countries was an enormous job. The Allies—France, England, and the United States— shared the responsibility with the UN Relief and Rehabilitation Agency to relocate 7 million refugees. Hundreds of doctors and nurses poured into Europe to help. Food and clothing were distributed. In the first five months after the war ended, the army had returned 5 million refugees to their homes. Most of the Jewish refugees, however, remained homeless.

In Poland, for example, of the 3.5 million Polish Jews alive before 1939, only 250,000 survived. But when they returned to their homes from the concentration or labor camps or from hiding in forests, they found they were unwelcome. Neighbors had taken their homes and land. Almost all of the refugees' relatives and friends had been killed. In addition, there were still attacks on Jews. In the first year after the war, five hundred Jews were murdered in Poland.

As a result, many of these refugees returned to the concentration camps, which were now called Displaced Persons camps. A year and a half after the war, there were still a million people in these camps who needed to find a home. The United States still did not want to let large numbers of Jews in. The frustration of the refugees in the camps led to many of them trying to illegally enter Israel, which was then Palestine and was governed by England. The trip was dangerous. Thousands of the refugees were arrested by the British and sent back to Europe. Finally, in 1948, three years after the war, Israel became a nation, and any Jew was allowed to become a citizen. At the same time, any remaining Jewish refugees who wished to were allowed to immigrate to the United States or Canada.

Top: All the wordly possessions of these Polish families are in the boxcar that is returning them to their homes after the war. Bottom: Polish refugees returning from Russia are deloused with DDT to prevent typhus epidemics. The United Nations supplied over 400 tons of DDT to Poland.

Top: In Italy, young refugees sleep on the street in a bed made from crates. Bottom left: This Polish family was driven from its farm by the Germans. When the family returned after the war, their house was destroyed, their livestock and tools were gone, and the land could no longer be cultivated. Bottom right: A woman and her grandchild who fled their home in Yugoslavia. Facing page: These Polish orphans are headed with their grandmother to a new home. The potatoes on the floor are all the food they have for their trip, which will last several days.

Top: These homeless Jews are survivors of a concentration camp in Poland, which after the war was turned into a Displaced Persons Camp. They are protesting because they want to go to Palestine, now Israel. Bottom: These Jewish refugees are walking across Europe. They are hoping to enter Palestine illegally. Facing page: This boat of refugees tried to go to Palestine but was captured by British soldiers.

A small child has lost her family in the crowds of fleeing refugees.

KOREA

FIVE

Korea, August 1951. Communist North Korea was at war with South Korea. UN forces from fifteen countries under U.S. command were fighting on the side of South Korea.

A unit of UN forces was retreating southward over the Naktong Bridge. Just behind the soldiers were thousands of Korean refugees pressed up against the bridge, trying to follow them to safety. The general in charge had orders to blow up the bridge. That way, the North Korean soldiers would not be able to cross the river. But the desperate refugees refused to remain on the other side. Each time the UN soldiers started across the bridge, a mass of refugees would follow. They tried to hold them back, but they couldn't. Finally, the general gave the order to blow up the bridge—with the refugees on it.

Soon after North Korea invaded South Korea in June 1950, millions of Koreans took to the roads. One million people alone left Seoul, the capital of South Korea. Most were just trying to escape from the bombs and fighting. Many were also afraid of living under Communist rule. Others were ordered to leave their homes by the South Korean army, who were afraid they would help the Communists.

Every road leading south was choked with people. Some traveled in old cars or in carts pulled by oxen. But most were forced to escape on foot. To protect themselves against the freezing cold, they wrapped their feet in rags and their bodies in blankets. Often, it was not enough. UN troops frequently stopped to rescue crying babies tied to the backs of their dead mothers lying on the side of the road.

Refugees also filled the railroad stations, hanging onto the sides of overflowing trains or waiting on the train tracks. Many were accidently hit by moving trains.

Pusan and other cities in the south became giant refugee camps. Several hundred thousand lucky refugees lived in camps set up by the United

Top: UN troops retreating from Suchon pass Korean refugees. Bottom: These people were ordered to leave by the South Korean army. Facing page: Korean refugees clamber over a bridge destroyed by bombs.

Top left: An American soldier checks a refugee's bundle for weapons. Top right: The last train packed with refugees pulls out of Suwon, South Korea as thousands of other refugees remain on the rails. Bottom: Thousands of people crossed the ice-covered Han river at Seoul.

Refugees from the North were interned in this tent city, searched for weapons, and given immunization shots.

Top: New arrivals at a refugee camp in South Korea. Bottom: Preparing a meal at a refugee camp in South Korea.

Nations. The majority slept in the streets or lived in shacks built of empty crates left behind as the UN army moved north or in cardboard huts not much bigger than a telephone booth. They survived on charity and food from private organizations, the American government, and the United Nations, which shipped grain, medical supplies, and clothing and set up homes for orphans and soup kitchens.

Here is what happened to two Korean boys, Son Hyun Ki, twelve, and Hwang Chon Man, thirteen, who were escaping with their families. Their story, told by a reporter in *Time* magazine, was not an unusual one.

> *When a packed refugee train from Seoul suddenly pulled out of the station at Taegu last winter, Son and Hwang were left behind on the platform, weeping and terrified. A trainman got them a ride southward to Pusan the next day. But when they arrived, half-frozen from the trip on a flatcar, they could nowhere find their families.*
>
> *Now six months later, Son and Hwang still scramble through the dirty streets of Pusan. There is almost nothing left of their neat primary-school uniforms. All Son wears is a blackened suit of underwear fastened around the shoulder with copper wire. They have no money. . . . They beg. They sleep in doorways, each noon go to the Pyongyang Noodle Shop, where the proprietor fills their pails with slops from the tables. Neither of them has a pair of shoes.*
>
> *. . . They have given up hope of finding their families. "Sometimes," Son said, "at first I used to dream of my mother holding out her arms to me. When it rains I still remember how it was on the warm floor at home."[5]*

When a truce was signed on July 27, 1951, there were 3.5 million refugees in South Korea. Fifty towns and 12,000 villages were completely destroyed. Although the refugees slowly rebuilt their homes and lives, they would never forget what happened to them. In nearly every family, a child or parent had died in the family's flight from war.

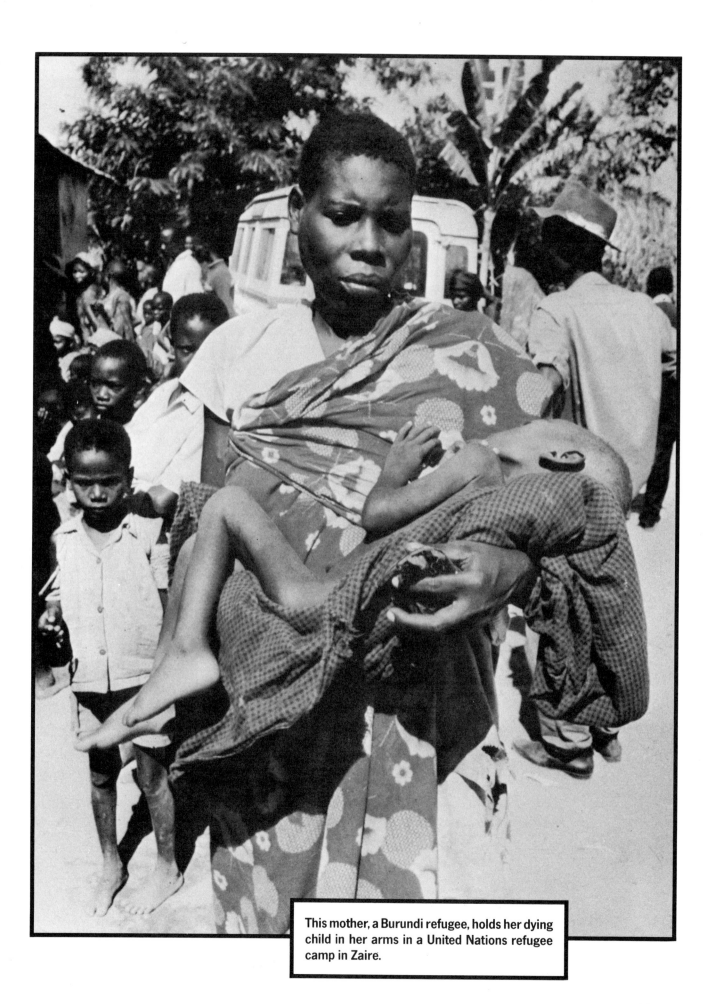

This mother, a Burundi refugee, holds her dying child in her arms in a United Nations refugee camp in Zaire.

AFRICA

SIX

Thirteen-year-old Judisi Sinduhije of Burundi, Africa, has a dream—to go to high school.

Judisi lives in a refugee camp run by the United Nations in Tanzania, a neighboring country of Burundi. The roof of the school that Judisi goes to is made of sheet metal, the floor is of earth, and the walls are bushes covered with mud. Judisi's desk is made from a tree trunk split in half.

After school, Judisi must get water for the family. She walks 1.5 miles (2.4 km) to the well and carries the water back in a bucket on her head. Then, reading by the light of a fire outside her home, she does her homework.

Although she works hard, Judisi's dream may never come true. It costs only about $50 a year to send a child to high school, but the community can afford to let only two of the fifty-five students in Judisi's class continue their schooling.

Judisi, whose family fled fighting in their homeland, is one of millions of refugee children in Africa. In the late 1980s, in Sudan alone, there were over 1.6 million refugees. In Mozambique, over a million people were uprooted from their homes because of war. But the numbers alone do not tell the story of their suffering. For most of modern history, Africa was ruled by European countries. But beginning in the 1960s, the nations of Africa gained their independence. Unfortunately, peace did not come to many of these newborn nations. Angola, for example, won independence from Portugal in 1975 after a thirteen-year guerrilla war. But as of 1988, the country was still at war—a civil war in which Angolans were fighting Angolans.

The refugees of Africa have fled terrible conditions. Children have seen their parents beaten or even brutally murdered by soldiers. Women have been raped. Homes have been destroyed. Tens of thousands of men, women, and children have been crippled by mines, bombs that are planted in the earth and explode when stepped on.

Amid all this suffering, there are the people who want to help. The United Nations has dozens of refugee camps in Africa that save lives and offer hope.

Numerous private organizations give money for food, clothing, and doctors, and students and other people from around the world have volunteered their skills and services. It is an enormous task.

To reach the UN camps, the refugees, many of whom are farmers, often leave their homes in small groups in the middle of the night. Although they may travel for several weeks to reach the refugee camp, they don't take much. Most of the time, they will be walking! On their way to the safety of the camps, the refugees may be attacked by wild animals or caught by the government army or rebels and be beaten or killed. To discourage refugees from escaping from neighboring war-torn Mozambique, South Africa built an electrified 10-foot (3-m)- high fence that can kill anyone who touches it.

When the refugees arrive at the camps, they are usually sick and starving. Their legs are often swollen, and their feet are torn by rocks. They may have lived for weeks on roots, leaves, and insects and be wearing old grain sacks for clothing. In most camps, the refugees can get food, water, and basic medical care and find shelter in a house made from pieces of wood or tree trunks. In some camps, though, home is a tent that offers no protection from wind or rain, and the bed is a piece of cardboard on the ground. Sometimes, refugees may find work in a neighboring village and have small gardens, and adults may be able to learn a trade.

But in all refugee camps, life is hard. There are no refrigerators, sinks, toilets, or even toys. Children play with tin cans and a piece of string.or use stones and beads to draw in the sand. Few African refugee children have ever seen a bicycle.

While the United Nations and other organizations hold out a hand, there are people who try to prevent the help from reaching the refugees. In Sudan, for example, rebel soldiers have stopped food shipments from relief organizations from coming to the refugee camp. In January 1988, a reporter from the *New York Times* described such a camp in Sudan:

> *...7,000 destitute people...Children with thin legs clung to mothers who were too weak to breast-feed. Men were emaciated, and few of them seemed to have the energy or will to do anything.*[6]

When fighting has stopped in their homelands, refugees are helped by the United Nations to go home. Sometimes, the refugees return to houses that have been destroyed. Wells must be repaired, roads are covered with tall grass, and farmlands may be infested with the dangerous tsetse fly. The United Nations gives the refugees seeds, tools, and construction materials. Although it is only a start, it is an important first step in helping these people to begin their lives again.

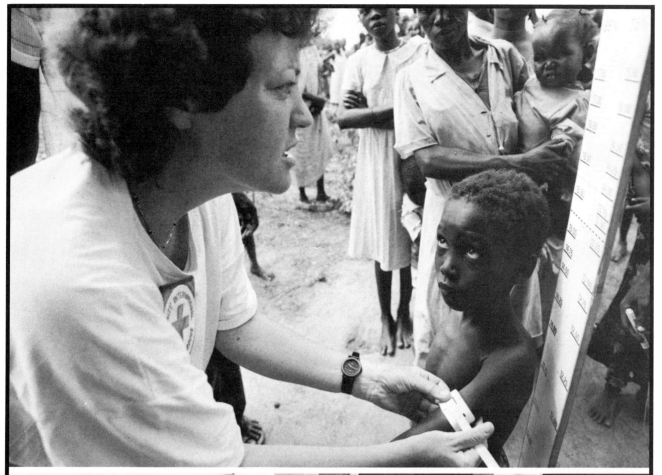

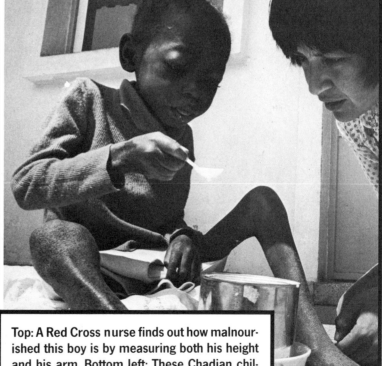

Top: A Red Cross nurse finds out how malnourished this boy is by measuring both his height and his arm. Bottom left: These Chadian children in a Sudan refugee camp search the sand for grains to eat. Bottom right: The intensive nutrition center at a hospital in Angola saved this boy's life. He was fed every three hours as well as given medical care.

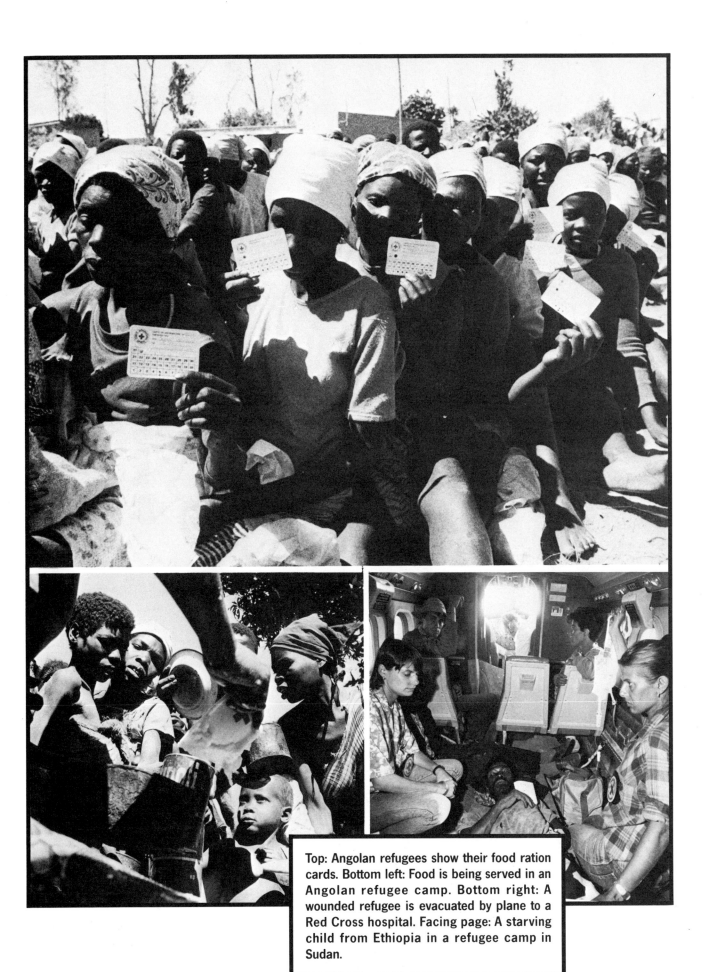

Top: Angolan refugees show their food ration cards. Bottom left: Food is being served in an Angolan refugee camp. Bottom right: A wounded refugee is evacuated by plane to a Red Cross hospital. Facing page: A starving child from Ethiopia in a refugee camp in Sudan.

Top: Tents were quickly put up in Rwanda to shelter Ugandan refugees. Bottom: Zimbabwean refugees in Botswana select clothes donated by UNICEF.

Top: Refugees from Rwanda pump water from a well in Uganda. Bottom: These Ethiopian women are building a house in a Somalian refugee camp.

Top: Rwandese refugees learn to sew in a camp in Burundi. Bottom: Rwandese children go to school in a refugee camp in Burundi.

REFUGIES TCHADIENS

HCR

CENTRE
D' INFORMATION ET DE RAPATRIEMENT

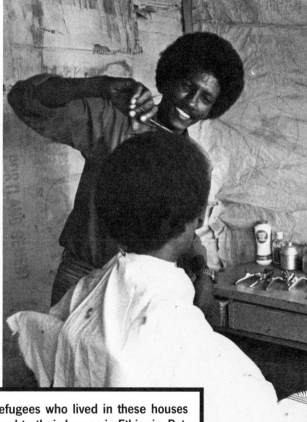

Top: The refugees who lived in these houses have returned to their homes in Ethiopia. Bottom left: Chadian refugees at a United Nations repatriation center wait to go home. Bottom right: An Ethiopian refugee has set up a barbershop in Port Sudan, a city in Sudan.

A boat packed with 162 Vietnamese refugees sinks a few meters off the shore of Malaysia.

SOUTHEAST ASIA

SEVEN

Sathaya Tor is from Cambodia. He is a refugee of war.

When Sathaya was seven years old, he was taken from his parents and sent to a child labor camp, where he was made to work all day. Children who cried were whipped. All he had to eat was two bowls of rice a day. After Vietnam invaded Cambodia in 1979, Sathaya escaped and made his way to a refugee camp in Thailand. He eventually came to the United States. Today, Sathaya is a student at Stanford University in California.

Lai Pham is from Vietnam. She is also a refugee of war.

When Lai was fourteen years old, she escaped on a small fishing boat crowded with other fleeing refugees after North Vietnam invaded South Vietnam. Soldiers shot at the escapees on the rickety craft as it desperately headed out to sea and the safety of an American boat.

Today, Lai lives in a suburb of Portland, Oregon. She is a draftsperson. Her husband, who is also a refugee from Vietnam, sells houses.

Since the mid-1970s, tens of thousands of men, women, and children like Sathaya and Lai have escaped war in Vietnam, Cambodia, and Laos and come to live in the United States and other countries. Like refugees before them, they have made countless contributions. They have opened up stores and restaurants, started their own businesses, and become computer operators, engineers, and scientists.

But many refugees from these countries torn by war remain in refugee camps throughout Southeast Asia. For them, the search for a permanent home has just begun.

For decades, war has been part of the landscape in this part of the world. From 1965 to 1973, the United States fought a controversial and undeclared war in Vietnam. They hoped to keep South Vietnam from becoming a Communist government like that of North Vietnam. During the war, as many as 6 million Vietnamese were displaced from their homes as they fled U.S. bombs and Communist forces. In slums around the major cities, two or three

Top: These Vietnamese refugees are trying to escape the fighting. Bottom: Vietnamese refugees climb from their fishing boat to a U.S. Naval ship.

Top left: Vietnamese in a refugee camp in Indonesia. Top right: Laotian refugee family of the Hmong tribe in a camp in Thailand. Bottom: A hospital in one of the largest refugee camps in Thailand.

families crowded into tiny sheds with tin roofs. Most were farmers and had no way to make a living. Some women were forced to become prostitutes; young children begged for or stole food.

When South Vietnam fell to the Communists in 1975, and American troops went home, many South Vietnamese wanted to leave with them. Those who had worked for the American government were afraid they would be killed by the Communists, and in the last few days before the end of the war, U.S. forces helped 132,000 refugees leave for the United States. But more wanted to go. There were heart-wrenching scenes of Vietnamese desperately hanging onto American helicopters as they took off and U.S. Marines beating back people trying to board airplanes. Some held onto the wheels and were crushed to death.

Throughout the late 1970s and early 1980s, many Vietnamese continued to try to escape in flimsy fishing boats. Dozens were drowned at sea, and women refugees were raped by pirates. Food ran out on the boats, which often got lost at sea. Some countries wouldn't let the boats land and towed them back to sea. But the refugees kept coming, cramming into refugee centers throughout Southeast Asia.

During the Vietnam War, other countries were drawn into the fighting. The North Vietnamese transported weapons through neighboring Cambodia, now known as Kampuchea. Although Cambodia was not involved in the conflict, the United States bombed the country. Angry at Vietnam, Cambodian soldiers attacked Vietnamese who lived in Cambodia. Thousands were killed. Tens of thousands became refugees, abandoning shops, homes, and farms and fleeing to Vietnam.

When the Communist leader, Pol Pot, and the Khmer Rouge took power in Cambodia, the stage was set for one of the most brutal governments in history. In three and a half years, the Khmer Rouge murdered nearly 2 million of Cambodia's 7 million people. Religion was banned, schools were abolished, and teachers were killed. There were no telephones and no postal services. Children were taken from their parents, and husbands and wives were separated.

Ouch Sarem, a Cambodian girl, once lived with her parents on a farm. In 1975, the Khmer Rouge took the farm and sent Ouch Sarem and her older brother and sister to a labor camp, where they worked from early morning to night mixing straw, leaves, and cow dung to make fertilizer. She was five years old. She saw her parents only once a week.

In 1979, when Vietnam invaded Cambodia, Ouch Sarem found her family. One day, soon after, they left their home at three in the morning,

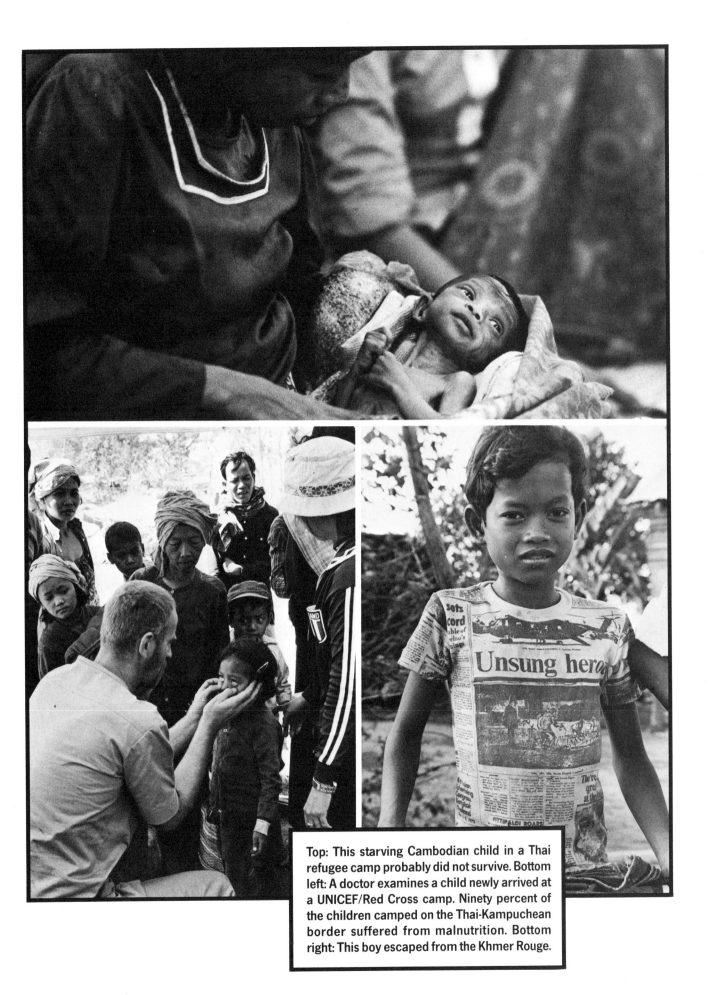

Top: This starving Cambodian child in a Thai refugee camp probably did not survive. Bottom left: A doctor examines a child newly arrived at a UNICEF/Red Cross camp. Ninety percent of the children camped on the Thai-Kampuchean border suffered from malnutrition. Bottom right: This boy escaped from the Khmer Rouge.

Top: Kampucheans who have just arrived at the UN camp wait for a medical checkup. Bottom left: Children on their way to school in a refugee camp in the Philippines. Bottom right: These Laotian refugees of the Yao tribe now live in a camp in Thailand.

meeting secretly to start their walk toward the Thai border. They traveled over mountain passes and streams, and slept on the ground at night. The trip to a refugee camp in Thailand took seven days.

Many refugees were not as lucky as Ouch Sarem and her family. Forty-two thousand refugees who entered Thailand were forced back into Cambodia. Those who resisted, including children, were shot. Others died from mines that exploded beneath their feet. There was no help for the wounded or dying. One survivor described her feelings:

> *The tears I thought were exhausted mounted to my eyes, less at the horror of that scene than at the idea that these innocent beings had paid with their lives for their attempt to find a place in a world too selfish to receive them.*[7]

Finally, the Thailand government decided to allow all refugees in—and 160,000 desperate Kampucheans entered the UN refugee camps.

Those who made it to the camps found medical help, food, and water. Schools were organized. Members of the Red Cross, the United Nations, and private relief organizations worked tirelessly to help the refugees.

Laos was also drawn into the Vietnam War. The North Vietnamese shipped weapons to soldiers in South Vietnam through Laos. The United States tried to stop this flow of arms by bombing Laos. By 1973, the bombs had made refugees of 700,000 Laotians.

During the war, the American army was helped by some of the Hmong, a hill tribe in Laos who also wanted to fight the Communists. When the Communists gained control of Laos, whole villages of Hmong tried to escape. But the Communist forces wanted revenge. They mined the roads to Thailand and killed escaping Hmong. Sometimes, it would take as long as six months for the refugees to get to the border. Men, women, and children lived on berries, roots, and insects. If someone became too sick to walk, he or she might be left behind, for if the group stayed to help, they might all be discovered and imprisoned. Some made it to the Mekong River, which divides Laos from Thailand, only to meet a tragic fate in the water, for many of these mountain people had never learned to swim. Others were pushed back into Laos by Thai soldiers.

Although hundreds of thousands of refugees have left the Thailand refugee camps for resettlement in the United States, Europe, Canada, and Australia, in the late 1980s there were still about 400,000 refugees in Thailand. Thousands of other refugees live in camps in Hong Kong and

Top: Vietnamese children play in Camp Pendleton, California. They live in the tents with their families. Bottom left: Cambodian, or Kampuchean, refugees in Indonesia learn a new language. Bottom right: This Vietnamese refugee, a former journalist, now works in an engine assembly plant in Switzerland.

Malaysia. The refugees in these camps are no longer hungry, but they now have other problems.

"We have met their physical needs," an aid worker in a camp in Thailand told a *New York Times* reporter, "but spiritually, they grow sicker."[8]

The refugees cannot leave the camp. Kids must make their own toys; there is little for adults to do. There are suicides, and crime is commonplace. Sometimes, fighting breaks out among different political groups in the Thai camps, and sometimes camps are attacked by artillery from Cambodia. In some camps, the refugees keep a few pots, some rice, and some clothes in a corner just in case they must flee.

But the tragedy for most of these refugees is that they have little to look forward to. They are not allowed to start a business or learn a trade because the countries in which they live do not want them to stay. Other countries don't want them, either. In most cases, refugees will only be admitted to a country if a close family member is already living there. Every day rejection letters are delivered to the camps. ". . . We have assessed that your prospects for successful settlement are not satisfactory," the letters say. "There is no appeal of this decision."

Near Bethlehem, a refugee family found shelter in a cave after fleeing their home in 1948 during the first Arab-Israeli conflict.

THE PALESTINIAN REFUGEES

EIGHT

In 1948, the day after Israel declared itself a nation, five neighboring Arab nations attacked it. During the fighting, over 700,000 Arabs who lived in the new state of Israel fled their homes. Some were sure the Israelis would lose the war and that they would be able to return to their homes in a week or two. Some were simply afraid or were encouraged by their leaders to leave. Still others were forced to leave their homes by the Israeli army. The largest number of refugees went to an area west of Israel along the Jordan River that is now called the West Bank. Others went to a strip of land along the Mediterranean Sea called the Gaza Strip, or to Jordan, Lebanon, and Syria.

Israel won the war. Three more wars followed—and more Arabs became refugees.

Most of the Palestinians who fled their country were able to find jobs and homes in neighboring Arab states. But one-third of the Palestinians continue to live in sixty-one refugee camps throughout the area.

These camps are often crowded. Some half-million people, for example, are squeezed into ten refugee camps in the Gaza Strip, which is only 6 miles (9.6 km) wide and 30 miles (48 km) long. A little over 200,000 Palestinian refugees live in twelve refugee camps in Jordan. Their homes are often tin shacks next to muddy alleyways. Other refugee camps have houses built of mud brick or concrete blocks. A typical house has two rooms and a cooking area. Most have bathrooms. There may also be tap water and sometimes electricity.

Although the United Nations has not been able to solve the Middle East conflict, it has given enormous help to the refugees. The UN Relief and Works Agency for Palestine Refugees in the Near East, or UNRWA, aids 2.1 million people in Jordan, Lebanon, Syria, the West Bank, and the Gaza Strip, providing schools, job-training programs, medical care, free lunches to children, milk powder for infants, and special rations for pregnant women and nursing mothers.

Top left: A refugee camp for Palestinians in Lebanon in 1952. A different family lived in each compartment. Top right: As they flee the war, these Palestinian girls push infant carts piled with household goods. Bottom: Immunization by a UNRWA doctor in East Jordan.

Top left: These Palestinian boys hold their ration cards in a refugee camp in the Gaza Strip. Top right: Mealtime in a refugee center in the Gaza Strip. Bottom: A refugee camp in Jordan after the 1973 War. These refugees fled from the Gaza Strip and the West Bank.

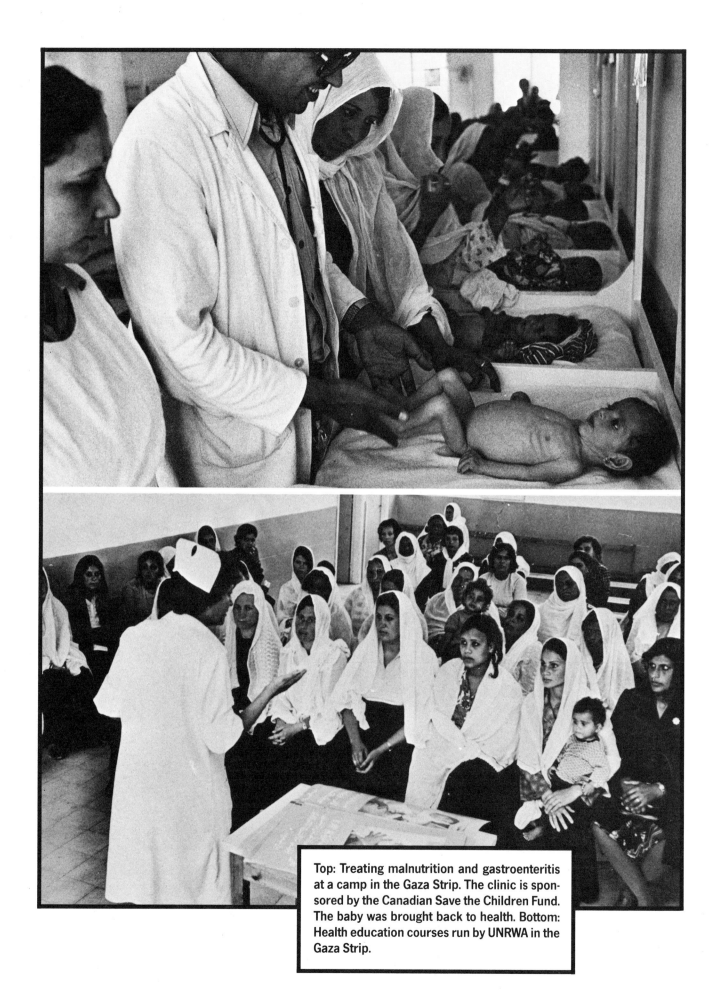

Top: Treating malnutrition and gastroenteritis at a camp in the Gaza Strip. The clinic is sponsored by the Canadian Save the Children Fund. The baby was brought back to health. Bottom: Health education courses run by UNRWA in the Gaza Strip.

Destruction of a refugee camp in Lebanon.
Water was brought in by UNRWA.

Top left: Palestinian women carry their belongings to a refugee camp. Top right: Palestinian refugees washing outside a tent. Bottom: Lining up for a meal in a refugee camp in Jordan.

To do its work, UNRWA must raise millions of dollars (only 4 percent of its $200 million budget comes from the United Nations). Most of the money comes from contributions from governments around the world, though there are also private organizations, church groups, business corporations, and private individuals who give. UNRWA has a staff of 17,500 men and women, including 10,160 teachers. Almost all the people helping the Palestinian refugees are Palestinians—and often refugees—themselves.

Israel is a democracy, but the Palestinian refugees who live on the West Bank and in Gaza do not enjoy the same rights as Israeli citizens. They cannot vote and be represented in the Israeli Parliament; they can be deported if they are suspected of encouraging people to riot; and their houses are destroyed if anyone in the family is suspected of terrorism. In the refugee camps of the Arab countries, which are not democracies, their lives are even more restricted. There, open political debate is forbidden and demonstrations are not allowed.

While Israel continues to build a modern, thriving society, the Palestinians feel increasingly frustrated. They want their own country on the West Bank and the Gaza Strip. Many Israelis are afraid that if they give the Palestinians back the land, the Palestinians and neighboring Arab countries will start another war with Israel. Some Israelis don't want to allow a Palestinian homeland simply because they want to keep the land for themselves.

In the 1970s and early 1980s, the Palestinians built up an army in the refugee camps in Lebanon. Soon, they were at war with their Lebanese hosts as well as Israel, which invaded Lebanon in return. The refugee camps were often attacked, and hundreds of innocent Palestinian refugees were killed, many more were injured, and some were once again driven from their homes.

By the end of the 1980s, the refugees were fighting Israeli soldiers on the West Bank and in Gaza. Angry young Palestinians threw stones at Israeli soldiers, who answered with beatings or bullets. At that time, it seemed that the future of the Palestinian refugees was a long way from being decided.

An old Afghan woman waits outside a medical aid center in a refugee camp in Pakistan.

AFGHANISTAN

NINE

Reza Gul is a young girl from Afghanistan. In 1985, her peaceful life came to an abrupt end.

Following a coup in 1979, which brought a Communist regime to power in Afghanistan, hundreds of thousands of refugees began to flee into neighboring Pakistan and Iran. Afghan rebels began a war against the new government. The rebels, or guerrillas, who are devout Moslems, hoped to end Communist control and establish a religious state. In the same year, Soviet troops invaded Afghanistan, and the number of refugees rose to the millions. By 1988, more than 5 million Afghan refugees were stranded outside their country, while another 2 million were homeless and displaced inside Afghanistan.

The war came to Reza's home one morning with the sound of screaming women and children, the screech of planes, and the boom of falling bombs exploding. People were killed or wounded as roofs caved in or as they ran into the street. Two of Reza's cousins died. Her family decided it was time to leave their home for the safety of refugee camps in Pakistan. They sold everything they owned and hired a camel. Then Reza, her mother, three brothers, and her grandparents packed a few small bags and, at night, started their trip. They traveled only in darkness through the steep mountain passes. It took four terrifying days.

Reza's new life in the refugee camp, with 15,000 other Afghans, is hard. Their house is made of mud. Three times a day, Reza must bring water to the house from a nearby spring. The family can rarely afford to buy meat.

Reza is one of nearly 2.5 million Afghan war refugees in Pakistan. Almost all are farmers or small-town artisans or shopkeepers. By the late 1980s, they were the largest single refugee population in the world. Other Afghans found safety in Iran, India, and Western Europe.

Many organizations from different countries have helped the Afghans. In some ways, the Afghan camps are better than refugee camps in other parts

Top: Children in an outdoor school in a refugee camp in Pakistan. Bottom left: Water is scarce in the refugee camps. Here, a baby is being bathed. Bottom right: Building a house from mud bricks.

Top left: A refugee boy wounded in the war learns to walk again in a Red Cross hospital in Pakistan. Top right: These Afghan refugees in Pakistan are of Turkmen origin. Bottom: Afghan boys in a refugee camp in Pakistan.

Top: New arrivals in an Afghan refugee camp in Iran. Bottom: A United Nations worker helps an elderly woman. Facing page: Prayer in an Afghan refugee camp.

Top left: Refugee families in Iran live in tents and rows of brick rooms. Top right: Children wait for their daily ration of milk. Bottom: These refugees from Afghanistan now live in France.

of the world. The refugees are free to leave the camp and look for work, and some have gone to cities or surrounding villages. Nevertheless, as in many relief operations, there are problems. Food is stolen, and the poor, the sick, women, and children are often the ones who do not receive enough food and supplies. For many years, there were no schools. Although schools for youngsters were finally started by the United Nations, there are still only four high schools. Also, many fewer girls go to school than boys, and the high schools are for boys only. Most devout Moslems do not believe girls should go to school after they are twelve years old. Many of the husbands of women with health problems do not allow their wives to be treated by male doctors, and some do not even want them to leave the house to be looked at by a female doctor. There are numerous cases of tuberculosis and malaria.

In the late 1980s, the Soviet Union began withdrawing its troops from Afghanistan. But the guerrillas say that they will keep fighting until all the Afghans who are Communists leave the government. In the meantime, Reza Gul sits in a refugee camp waiting to go home.

Two Guatemalan girls in a refugee camp in Mexico clutch their only toys.

CENTRAL AMERICA

TEN

Americans often take living in their country for granted. But for millions of people around the world, moving to the United States is a lifelong dream. For some refugees from Central America, it's a matter of life or death.

The countries of El Salvador, Guatemala, and Nicaragua are desperately poor. Most of the people are farmers, but few own their land. In Guatemala, for example, more than half the good farmland is owned by only 3 percent of the people. The average income in El Salvador is only $2,500 a year. In Nicaragua, there is often not enough food in stores.

Until the early 1980s, all these countries were run by dictators. Violence was a way of life. In El Salvador, people would disappear daily. Torture and death at the hands of the army or paramilitary "death squads" was not uncommon.

In the last decade, war has brought more suffering. Thousands of people have died; more have fled their homelands. Many of the refugees say that if they return home, they will be killed by government soldiers or guerrillas fighting the government and have asked the United States for asylum. The United States, which supports the governments of Guatemala and El Salvador, usually refuses and throughout the 1980s forced thousands of Guatemalans and Salvadorans to return home each year. Many go into hiding; there may be as many as 500,000 Salvadorans and 100,000 Guatemalans living in the United States illegally. Because refugees live in fear of being found by the police, employers often take advantage of them and pay them very little money for their work.

To gain asylum in the United States, one must prove a "well-founded fear of persecution on account of race, religion, nationality, membership in a particular social group, or political opinion." The U.S. government claims that these refugees are not in danger of being persecuted if they go home. Instead, they say, the refugees want to come to the United States to better themselves financially. Some American citizens disagree and have even been willing to go to jail for their beliefs.

Top: Guatemalan women get water from a well in a refugee camp in Mexico. Bottom: Youngsters from El Salvador watch tortillas being made in a refugee camp in Honduras. Facing page: These refugees traveled nearly 14 hours to be relocated away from the border and further inside Mexico, where they will be safer.

Top: A camp for refugees from El Salvador in Honduras. Refugees are not allowed to leave the camp. Bottom left: Refugees line up for food. Bottom right: Guatemalan women refugees carry water back to their camp in earthen pots.

Top: Communal cooking in a refugee camp in Mexico. Bottom: These Guatemalan refugees earn money by weaving.

The Sanctuary Movement, for example, an organization of more than four hundred churches and synagogues that was started in 1982, provides aid to refugees from El Salvador and Guatemala who say they are being persecuted by their governments. In 1986, in a trial in Tucson, Arizona, eight nuns and priests were found guilty of helping refugees from Central America. Some U.S. cities have even adopted "noncompliance" and won't aid federal government officials in locating refugees who are not here legally.

A law passed by Congress in 1986 offered legal status or amnesty to illegal aliens who could prove that they had been living in the United States since 1982. Many Central American refugees applied for amnesty under this law.

Not all Central American refugees, however, come to the United States. Instead, they escape across the border to a neighboring country or become refugees in their own land.

In the 1980s, some 250,000 refugees from El Salvador fled the war between guerrillas and the government. They went to Honduras, Mexico, and Costa Rica.

The refugees often arrive in the camps with infections from falls or cuts on their feet. Women have been raped by soldiers. Everyone is thirsty, hungry, exhausted, and frightened. In 1980, as many as six hundred Salvadoran refugees were massacred as they tried to cross into Honduras. They were fired on by both Salvadoran and Honduran soldiers. Another 400,000 people who lived in the countryside escaped bombings by the government and violence by the guerrillas by moving to San Salvador, the capital. The conditions in these refugee camps are terrible. Children have head lice, are sick, and don't have enough to eat.

The refugees who decide to go home can be putting themselves in great danger. In 1987, for example, 4,335 refugees went back to El Salvador. Their homes were in an area of the country that was under the influence of the guerrillas. The government, afraid that the refugees might help the guerrillas, bombed one of these towns. It was a warning sign. But the refugees didn't leave. They returned to their destroyed houses and overgrown fields and tried to start their lives anew.

The people of Guatemala are also on the run. In its attempt to wipe out a small group of guerrillas, the Guatemalan army has terrorized the population, destroying hundreds of villages and torturing and killing thousands of people, often including teachers and other community leaders who they fear will turn the people against them. The guerrillas also threaten and kill people.

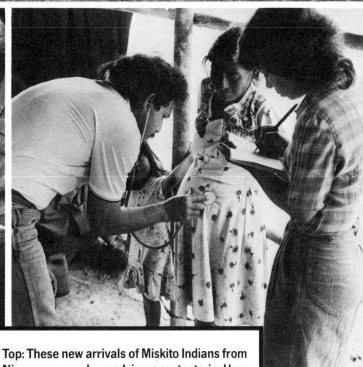

Top: These new arrivals of Miskito Indians from Nicaragua are housed in open tents in Honduras. Bottom left: A Miskito Indian family in Honduras. Bottom right: A UNICEF doctor examines a Guatemalan refugee.

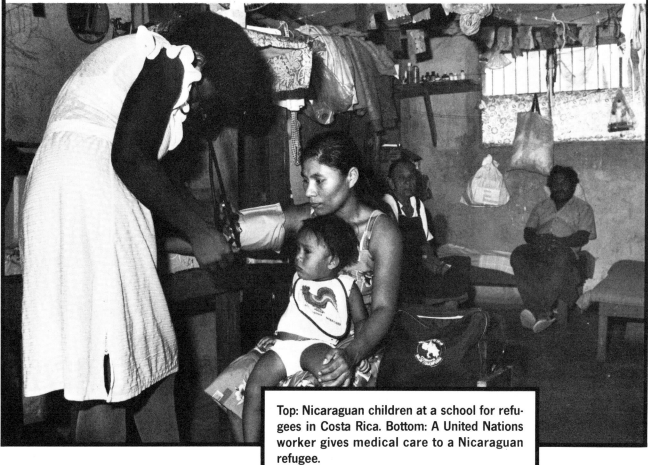

Top: Nicaraguan children at a school for refugees in Costa Rica. Bottom: A United Nations worker gives medical care to a Nicaraguan refugee.

To escape the violence, 45,000 Guatemalans have fled to Mexico; others have gone to Belize, Honduras, Nicaragua, and Costa Rica.

The Nicaraguans, led by a group called the Sandinistas, overthrew their dictator in 1979. But there is still no peace in that country, either. Former members of the dictator's army, as well as other Nicaraguans who do not like the new leaders, are waging a guerrilla war. Called the Contras, they have been given money, weapons, and medical supplies by the U.S. government. The Contras fight along the Honduran and the Costa Rican borders, and the people who live in that region are caught in the crossfire.

"The Contras come with guns and take away our food," complains one Nicaraguan woman in an area near the fighting. "Then the Sandinistas come and arrest us because they say we work for the Contras."[9]

Almost 4,000 peasants have moved from their homes to protected government settlements. Some did it on their own; others moved on orders of Sandinista troops. Altogether, perhaps some 250,000 Nicaraguans are displaced within their own country. Thousands of Miskito Indians were expelled from their villages along the Honduran border in late 1981. Sandinista troops burned many of the villages to prevent them from becoming bases for the Indians who, they believed, were helping the Contras. In 1986, another 10,000 Indians fled to Honduras to escape the fighting between the Contras and the Nicaraguan government.

It is estimated that about 200,000 Nicaraguans are in Costa Rica and Honduras, and another 200,000 may be in the United States, Mexico, and other Latin American countries.

Life in the refugee camps in Central America varies. Home may be a small wooden house that two or three families share, and there is little or no privacy. The camps often have shops where the refugees work at hammock-making, tailoring, carpentry, shoemaking, or embroidery. There are health clinics and schools for the young children. Women may spend their days carrying fuel and water to the house and taking care of the children. The children build toys from sticks. There are few, if any, dolls to play with.

In some camps in Honduras where Salvadoran refugees live, there may be as few as thirty bathrooms for a thousand people, and there are long lines to get water. Breakfast, which is tortillas, fried beans, and rice, is eaten at 6:30 every morning. Lunch is beans, rice, tortillas, and eggs. Dinner is at 5:00 and is similar to lunch. Fruit is a rarity. In these camps, the refugees are in some ways like prisoners, for nobody can leave the camp unless that person is sick and needs to go to a hospital.

Many of the refugees who go to Costa Rica, the only stable democracy in Central America, move to cities and towns. There, they are helped by the Costa Rican Red Cross and other humanitarian organizations that provide housing, food, education, and health care. They also are helped in finding work. The camps of refugees in the countryside are often overcrowded, and although the housing is often not good, the refugees have enough to eat and medical care.

But even if they feel safe and are well fed, refugees are always missing "something." Here's how a Salvadoran refugee who lives in a camp in Honduras describes that "something":

We are always thinking about our country, El Salvador ... where we left our friends, brothers and sisters, our relatives; and also where we left our crops and all our belongings.

When evening comes, we feel the saddest, because we know that one more day has passed and we are still far from our country ... [10]

NOTES

1. J. Missakian, *A Searchlight on the Armenian Question* (Boston: Hairenek Publishing Co., 1950), p. 41.

2. Michael R. Marrus, *The Unwanted: European Refugees in the Twentieth Century* (New York: Oxford University Press, 1985), p. 80.

3. "Caring for Thousands of Refugees," *The New York Times Current History Magazine* (May 18, 1918), pp. 228–29.

4. Michael R. Marrus, *The Unwanted: European Refugees in the Twentieth Century* (New York: Oxford University Press, 1985), p. 62.

5. "The Forgotten People," *Time Magazine* (July 16, 1951), p. 23.

6. "War and Drought Inflicting Famine in Sudan," *The New York Times* (January 3, 1988), p. 15.

7. Joan D. Criddle and Teeda Butt Mam, *To Destroy You Is No Loss: The Odyssey of a Cambodian Family* (Boston: The Atlantic Monthly Press, 1987), p. 255.

8. Barbara Crossette, "Trapped at Thai Camps, Cambodians Despair," *The New York Times* (September 21, 1987), p. 14.

9. Stephen Kinzer, "Contras Are Reported to Establish a Foothold in Central Nicaragua," *The New York Times* (September 13, 1987), p. 24.

10. Renato Camarda, *Forced to Move* (San Francisco: Solidarity Publications, 1985), p. 49.

FURTHER READING

Bentley, Judith. *Refugees: Search for a Haven.* New York: Messner, 1986.

Frank, Anne. *Diary of a Young Girl.* New York: Doubleday, 1967.

Heaps, Leo. *A Boy Called Nam.* Toronto: Macmillan, 1984.

Loescher, Gil. *The World's Refugees.* San Diego: Harcourt Brace Jovanovich, 1982.

Marrus, Michael R. *The Unwanted: European Refugees in the Twentieth Century.* New York: Oxford University Press, 1985.

McDowall, David. *The Palestinians.* New York: Gloucester Press, 1986.

Stone, Scott C. S., and John E. McGowan. *Wrapped in the Wind's Shawl: Refugees of Southeast Asia and the Western World.* San Rafael, California: Presido Press, 1980.

World Refugee Survey: 1986 in Review. Washington, D.C.: U.S. Committee for Refugees, 1987.

INDEX